ILLUSTRATED GUIDE OF ASSISI

Translated by Benedict Fagone

S C
C.E.F.A.
Assisi - Casa Editrice Francescana dei Frati Minori Conventuali
Umbriagraf - Terni

GIOTTO The sermon to the birds (Detail)

“GOD bless you, holy city, because many souls will be saved through you, and in you will dwell servants of the Most High, from you many will be chosen for the eternal kingdom”.

INDEX

HISTORY, ARTISTIC EXCELLENCE, SPIRITUALITY OF THE BASILICA OF ST. FRANCIS

HISTORICAL ORIGINS

EARLY ORIGINS. The early origins of Assisi date back to the time of the Etruscans and of the Roman Empire. From that period there still remain several noteworthy monuments, such as the façade of the temple of Minerva (today the church of Santa Maria sopra Minerva), traces of a theatre and an amphitheatre in the upper part of the town, some ruins of the Forum, as well as some parts of the ancient walls of the city.

MEDIEVAL ASSISI. During the early Middle Ages Assisi was often the scene of strife and civil war. In 1202 Perugia overcame the forces defending Assisi and took many prisoners, among whom also Francis Bernardone. For several centuries the city continued to be the scene of conflict as it passed from the hands of one ruler to another. Finally Pope Paul III (1534-1549) placed the city under papal dominion which lasted until the occupation by the Italian government in 1870.

Although other cities in Italy may likewise bear a medieval imprint and contain many artistic treasures, Assisi is famous the world over because it is the birthplace of Francis of Assisi, because his body lies buried in the great Basilica erected in his honor, because his spirit, hovering somehow over this city he blessed, attracts and inspires people of all creeds and nations. His close imitation of Christ, his heroic dedication to the ideals he espoused carry a message to men of all centuries eager to live in peace, in justice, and brotherly love. St. Clare of Assisi, whose remains are buried in the church bearing her name, foundress of the Poor Clares under the direction of Francis, adds to the lustre of this Umbrian city.

1. LIFE OF ST. FRANCIS. Francis was born in Assisi during the winter of 1181-1182. His father, Peter Bernardone, a cloth merchant, was on a business trip at the time. His mother, Giovanna called la Pica had her son baptized John; but when his father returned, he changed his son's name to Francis. Different opinions are advanced regarding the location of the home of the Bernardone family. According to a tradition, however, Francis was born in the stable, which most probably was located on the spot where the Oratory of Little Francis (Oratorio di Francesco Piccolino) now stands.
In his youthful years Francis seems to have had plenty of money to spend, and enjoyed good times with the group that associated with him. He became enthusiastic about a military career, and so, fully equipped, he set off for southern Italy. By the grace of God he came to realize this was not to be his calling; so very shortly he went back to Assisi. This occurred in 1205. He resumed for a time his former carefree life. Returning home a festive evening, Francis told his friends he was in love with a most noble bride, for he felt inspired to espouse a life of poverty. He began to spend much time in prayer and wanted to share his earthly possessions with the poor. He desired to be poor like Christ. One day while praying before the Crucifix in the dilapidated church of St. Damian, he heard these words: «Francis, go and repair my church which you see is falling into ruin». Because he did not realize until later that he was called to effect a spiritual restoration, he immediately began to gather materials; and to raise money he took cloth from his father's store,

went to Foligno where he sold the cloth and his horse and he gave the money to the priest at St. Damian. His angry father took up the matter with the authorities. Father and son appeared before the Bishop and a gathering of people. Francis stripped off his own clothes and gave them back to his father, saying: «Until now I have called Peter Bernardone my father. From now on I shall say: Our Father in heaven». God alone would now provide for his spiritual and even material needs. It was a turning point in his life.

Appalled by the injustice in the world because of greed and the avid desire of wealth to the neglect of the poor, Francis had renouced his paternal inheritance to embrace the life of the poor under the fatherhood of God. In search of his way of life, he one day read the Gospel: «Take no gold, nor silver, nor copper in your belts, no bag for your journey, nor two tunics, nor sandals, nor a staff...» and in the Gospel he established his Franciscan program, the Rule he and his followers observed. From that time — as he records in his Last Testament — «those things which at first seemed so attractive, so pleasant and enjoyable, became entirely unattractive, undesirable, even disagreable; on the contrary things which previously had been repulsive to him became desirable, a source of joy. No longer did he shun lepers; he embraced them and bound up their wounds.

The origins of the Franciscan movement read like an epic poem. It begins with that heroic period of the poor and austere life at Rivotorto where the first eleven disciples gathered around Francis, where with the approval by Pope Innocent III of the Rule of life the Franciscan movement was born. Thereafter the friars set forth from the Porziuncola, where Francis and his followers lived from 1211, on their apostolic missions. It was at the Porziuncola also that Clare of Assisi began her life of consecration to God; later (1212) she founded the Poor Clares — the Second Order of St. Francis. True to their missionary calling, the friars set forth in 1213-1214 to preach the Gospel in foreign lands, a mission in which Francis personally took part. To stir the faithful to prayer and repentance, Francis obtained in 1216 the Porziuncola indulgence. The increase in membership was both rapid and impressive, so much so that when the first great Chapter of administration and discipline convened, thousands of friars assembled.

From 1221 a new phase opens in the life of the Poverello: whereas he had previously devoted most of his time to his fellowmen, thereafter he began to spend more and more time in secluded prayer, penance and contemplation. It was on Sept. 17, 1224 after a period of particularly intense prayer and penance on Monte Verna (not far from Arezzo), which drew him into ever deeper intimacy with his Crucified Savior, Francis received the marks of the sacred stigmata, or wounds of Christ Crucified, on his hands and feet and in his side.

2. SANTUARIO DI S. FRANCESCO

ARCHITECTURE AND DESIGNER. The church of St. Francis in Assisi, the cathedral in Siena are the first examples of this individual characterization of Italian Gothic. Similar to the first literary efforts in the vernacular, after a certain period of hesitancy, of hybrid forms in respect to the poetry introduced from France which arose eventually to the creative level of a Dante Alighieri, so too the uncertain, indefinite initial character of the Gothic developed somewhat in Italy into the masterpiece of this church in Assisi. It was the first in the series of sacred and non-sacred edifices costructed in Italy as a result of the preceding somewhat disorientated tendencies between the old and the new, between the imported pure Gothic and the modified Italian Gothic.

In March 1228, only eighteen months after the death of the Poverello, Simone di Pucciarello, a resident of Assisi, donated to the friars, who accepted it on the authority of Pope Gregory IX, the hill situated to the west below the city called the lower hill by reason of its position. Legend has it that this area, infamous because it was a place of public execution of malefactors, was chosen by Francis who considered himself the worst sinner, as his burial place. In 1228 Monaldo di Leonardo donated to the friars the wooded area on the northern slope of this hill.

On July 16, 1228 Pope Gregory IX declared Francis a saint and the following day blessed the cornerstone and placed it upon the hill which he christened the hill of Paradise. In this church to be constructed there, the remains of St. Francis were to be buried (his remains had previously been taken to the church of St. George). On May 25, 1230 the body of the Saint was placed in a stone sarcophagus which was embedded in the solid rock beneath the main altar. Within

Basilica of St. Francis

only two years the crypt, known at that time as the lower church, was constructed. Since by 1236 the great Crucifix by Giunta Pisano had been completed for erection in the upper church, and by 1239 the bell tower had been completed and the bells cast, it may be logically inferred that about this time the upper church had been completed.
After May 1253, consequent upon the «Brief» of Pope Innocent IV who had come to consecrate the church, the decorative work on the interior was resumed. From 1269 onwards, when Assisi began to be the center of throngs of pilgrims eager to acquire the Porziuncola Indulgence of Pardon, the entry transept was enlarged and the side chapels of the lower church were constructed.
Beyond a doubt, Brother Elias the beloved disciple of St. Francis, of whom he was Vicar and subsequently the second Minister General of the Franciscan Order, conceived the plan of this structure. He spared no effort to obtain the cooperation of all the friars of the Order in order to create the grandiose Basilica desired

LOWER BASILICA OF ST. FRANCIS

1 Entrance to the Lower Basilica
2 Relics
3 Old Cemetery of the Franciscans
4 Entrance to the Tomb of the Saint
5 Chapel of St. Martin
6 Chapel of St. M. Magdalen
7 Madonna and St. Francis (Cimabue)
8 Main Altar and Allegories (Giotto)
9 Madonna of Sunset (P. Lorenzetti)
10 Sacristy
11 Cloister of Sixtus IV and internal entrance to the Upper Basilica

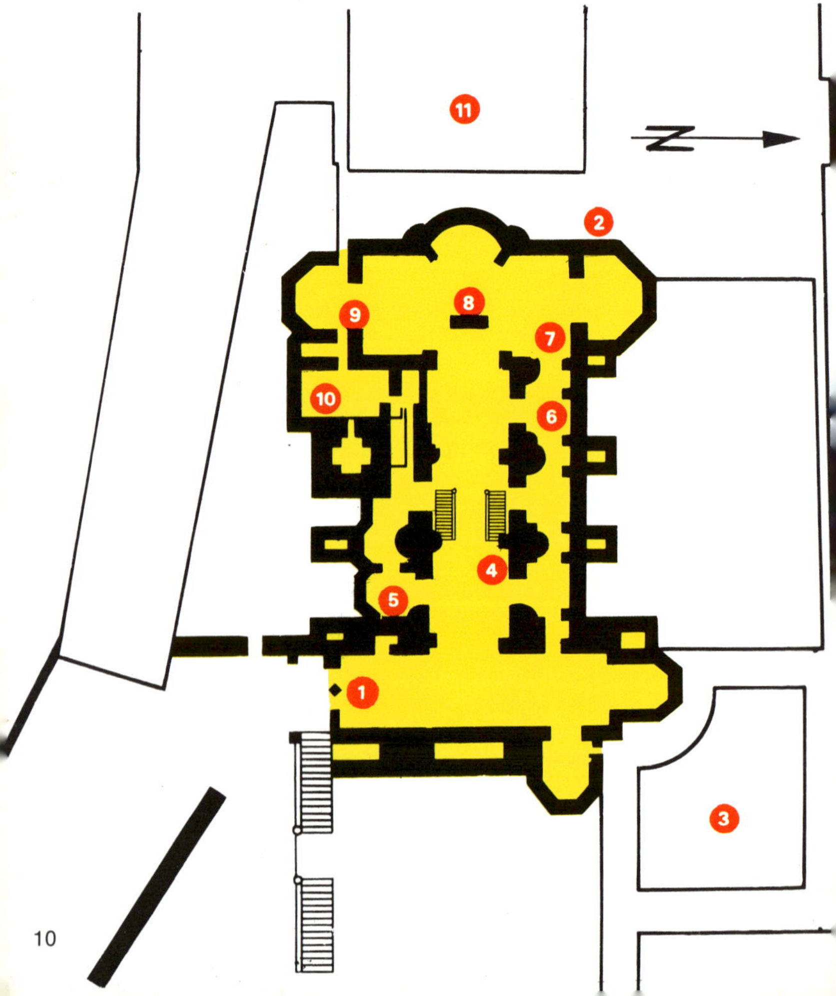

UPPER BASILICA

LOWER BASILICA

CRYPT

by the Pope and the entire Church to honor the sanctity of the Poverello. Absolutely unfounded, as recent resarch has revealed, are the assertions made by the rebellious so-called Spirituals of the XIV century that dissensions arose between Brother Elias and the other disciples of Francis because of the grandeur of this sacred edifice.

The land on which the church was to be built was the exclusive property of the Holy See. In October 1228 Gregory IX proclaimed it to be directly dependent upon Rome by accepting the land as property of the Holy See; in 1230, after the lower church had been completed, he reaffirmed this title of ownership. He likewise designated this church the head and mother of all Franciscan Churches. His successors repeatedly confirmed these pontifical rights.

Pope Benedict XIV decreed in the Apostolic Costitution he issued on March 25, 1754 that on an equal plane with the major Roman Basilicas, St. Peter's, the Lateran, St. Mary Major, St. Paul and St. Lawrence in Campo Verano, the church of St. Francis in Assisi should have the title with respective rights and privileges of a Patriarchal Basilica and Papal Chapel. This sanctuary in Assisi therefore is not only the property of the Pope and subject to him alone, but as a Cappella Papale it is also a place in which the liturgy is celebrated by the direct authority of the Pope with that solemnity and decor proper to be observed by those who perform and assist at the ceremonies celebrated by the Pope or in his august presence.

ARTISTIC TREASURES. Beyond the spiritual treasures with which this Franciscan Basilica has been enriched and adorned in abundance and quality not accorded perhaps to any other Italian church, it is a monument to Italian architecture, a temple most artistically adorned. In constructing and decorating this structure there concurred not only friars skilled in works of art, but also extremely skilled workers in Comacene and Cosmatesque decorative art, and builders trained in Gothic construction and local lapidary work. Above all triumph the paintings of the thirteenth and fourteenth century which decorate all the walls and give the edifice its distinctive Italian character.

The name of the first artist who decorated the nave of the lower church is unknown. He is called Maestro di S. Francesco. In his art work, done around the middle of the thirteenth century, it is held that he was a pupil of Giunta Pisano. To this same Maestro di S. Francesco is ascribed the great Crucifix, a work done for the upper church, subsequently lost, on which there was this inscription: «Brother Elias ordered this work done. Christ Jesus have mercy on Brother Elias who prays; Giunta Pisano painted me, A.D. 1236». Then came the triumphant, vigorous and dramatic style of Cenni di Pepo, called Cimabue, the most renowned Florentine painter before Giotto. Almost contemporaneously the Roman painters Jacopo Torriti and Filippo Rusuti working in the upper church began to give expression to that Romanesque originality which finally grew out of their work. In this phase of development Giotto entered, the great master who was to epitomize in his masterpieces (among which, certain frescoes are in Assisi) the artistic painting being done in the central region of Italy, thus unifying the various local and Romanesque traditional trends. Among the painters in the school of Giotto, mention may be made of Maso, and Stefano, but the renowned are the Sienese masters of the fourteenth century: Simone Martini and Pietro Lorenzetti, outstanding for their «expressionism» so diverse and personal but obedient to that rigorous style which produced their true works of art.

SACRO CONVENTO. The convent which flanks the south side and apse of the Basilica was constructed partly contemporaneously with the church, and partly in later periods. It embraces also a section called the Papal Apartments used occasionally by Popes. Toward the begining of the fourteenth century it began to be called Sacro Convento, a name retained to this day. The original structure of three wings, symmetrical with the apse of the Basilica, was enlarged already in the thirteenth century by means of massive supporting walls and arches and a long portico having on the south side a series of Romanesque and Gothic arches. Thus as one approaches Assisi from the Umbrian valley, the long series of superimposed arches is very impressive. On the western side of the convent toward Perugia, structures were raised upon those already existing, and sloping constructions of reinforcement were added; thus another section was added to the convent, which served as an infirmary. Sixtus IV in the fifteeenth century had the great cloister renovated and ordered work done on the western wall of Sacro Convento, to which dates the present appearance of that part.

VISIT TO THE BASILICA

LOWER CHURCH

LOWER SQUARE.

The long low arcade or portico surrounding the lower square of San Francesco dates back to the fifteenth century. While camping beneath this portico in days past, pilgrims had fastened their beasts to the rings embedded in its walls. They can still be seen today on these walls.
Opposite the entrance to the lower church is the Oratory of St. Bernardine of Siena. In the arch above its two doors can be seen St. Bernardine between two angels (1488).
The double entrance door of the lower church, richly decorated in stone and marble (dating back to the thirteenth century, prior to Giotto) is surmounted by a large rose window flanked by two smaller ones. The protiro or porch which protects the windows is the work of Francesco di Pietrasanta (1487); the wooden imposts of the doors on the left were done by Ugolinuccio da Gubbio (c. 1550), and those of the right by an unknown artist (1573). They contain stories (from top to bottom and from left to right) taken from the life of St. Francis, St. Clare, St. Louis, St. Anthony. On the left wall is a bust of Pope Benedict XIV who conferred the privilege of Patriarchal Basilica and Cappella Papale upon the church of St. Francis.

ENTRANCE TRANSEPT. Passing through the door of the lower church one arrives at the entrance transept, the first and third part of which were added about 1271 to the original church.

rticato (XIIIth cent.)

Portal of the Lower Church

LEFT SIDE

Small chapel of St. Sebastian. Above the altar: St. Sebastian (painted by Sermei in the seventeenth century; on the left, Irene taking care of St. Sebastian (done by Martelli c. 1646); on the right, St. Sebastian before Domitian (by Martelli).
On the left wall of the entrance to this chapel: the images of Our Lady of Good Health, St. Anthony the abbot, St. Francis, and St. Rufinus the bishop of Assisi, paintings done by Ottaviano Nelli in the fifteenth century. Likewise on the left is a painting of St. Christopher done by the Umbrian school in the fourteenth century.

RIGHT SIDE

In the first span: Burial sepulcher monument to the memory of Giovanni dei Cerchi; surmounted by a vase made of porphyry, the gift of a queen of Cyprus donated about the begining of the fourteenth century. In the second section: a Tribune by a local sculptor of the fourteenth century, decorated with maiolica, dating from 1458; the parapet is of the seventeenth century; finally there is a burial monument to the memory of Giovanni di Brienne. Above it and to the right we find a statue of the Blessed Virgin; at the left a figure of a young woman wearing a crown seated upon a lion — the work of a certain Cosmatesco about the year 1290 (a rough copy of the style of Arnolfo).
The arch between the first and second sections, the walls and vault of the third section of this entrance transept were frescoed by Sermei (1645), assisted by Martelli. These scenes, in a bad state of deterioration, represent the mysteries of the Redemption, figures of prophets and saints.

Old Cemetery of XVth century

Statue of St. Francis by Father Luigi Sapia OFM Conv. (1925) in old cementery

CHAPEL OF ST. ANTHONY ABBOT. This is the right side of the third section of this transept. In the niches of the walls are the burial monuments in memory of Blasco Fernandez and his son Gracia, slain during a visit in the duchy of Spoleto in 1367. This is the work of a local artist of the fourteenth century.

FRIARS' CEMETERY. Access to this cemetery is through the chapel of St. Anthony, Abbot. This small remanesque-gothic cloister and its two loggias was built in the fourteenth century and enlarged in the fifteenth. The silence of the enclosure speaks of the profound peace preached by St. Francis. Through the grilled gate one has a view of the north side of the Basilica and the monastery garden.

CHAPEL OF ST. CATHERINE. In the apse of the entrance transept is the chapel dedicated to St. Catherine of Alexandria, Martyr. Erected about 1270, it was later enlarged and completely decorated at the expense of Cardinal Egidio Albornoz († 1367)

whose body was buried here but afterwards transferred to Toledo, Spain. About the year 1368 Andrew of Bologna painted above the high marble sacle the eight frescoes which depict scenes from the life of St. Catherine: (beginning from below and proceding upwards, on the right wall) 1) Conversion of St. Catherine, 2) The Saint before the emperor Maximinus, 3) The philosophers whom the Saint confuted are condemned to death at the stake by the Emperor, 4) The dispute with the pagan philosophers in the presence of Maxentius, 5) In prison St. Catherine converts the Empress Faustina, and the Saint receives food from the angels, 6) Martyrdom of Faustina, 7) St. Catherine is delivered from the torture of the wheel, 8) The Saint is beheaded, and the angels transfer her body to Mt. Sinai.
The decorations, the figures of saints seated in the splay, the beveled walls of the windows, the frescoes of St. Blase, St. Eugene, St. Louis, Rufinus (?), St. Clement, and St. Francis are also the work of Andrew of Bologna.
The stained glass of the three windows, depicting various saints, is the work of Giovanni di Bonino of Assisi, done about the middle of the fourteenth century.
Above the altar hangs a wooden crucifix by an anonymous sculptor of the fifteenth century.

CRYPT OR TOMB OF ST. FRANCIS

Access to the crypt is by way of two lateral stairways down the central nave of the lower church. Here in a roughly hewn stone sarcophagus, contained within the large open pillar in the center of the cruciform crypt are the sacred remains of the Poverello. In this very spot in 1230 Brother Elias hid the body of Francis making it inacessible and safe from any violation. In 1818, after 52 nights of digging, the Friars of Sacro Convento, authorized by Pope Pius VII, opened up the area in which the stone sarcophagus lay. In 1820 the crypt hewed out of the solid rock was completed and open to the public. The neoclassic style in which the crypt had been constructed was replaced in 1932 by the design of the architect Ugo Tarchi in the actual form it has today. In the niches at each angle facing the tomb lie buried the bodies of four disciples of Francis, fra Leone, fra Masseo, fra Rufino, and fra Angelo, which four had previously been buried in the lower church.

The tomb of St. Francis

At the landing where the dual staircase unites, just before descending to the level of the crypt, are the remains of the noblewoman, Blessed Jacopa dei Settesoli, a devout benefactress of St. Francis who called her Frate Jacopa.
At the entrance to the crypt, suspended from the vault, is the votive lamp which burns constantly before the tomb of Francis, the patron of Italy.

SIDE CHAPELS OF THE NAVE

CHAPEL OF ST. MARTIN. The first chapel on the left of this central nave is dedicated to St. Martin. It was decorated through the generosity of Cardinal Gentile Partino da Montefiore (d. 1312) a Franciscan. The frescoes are by Simone Martini (prior to 1317) and they portray ten salient episodes in the life of St. Martin. Going from left to right and proceeding from the lower to the higher paintings the following scenes are depicted: 1) St. Martin gives alms, 2) The dream of St. Martin, 3) The investiture of the Saint, 4) St. Martin abandons the military career, 5) St. Martin resuscitates a child, 6) St. Martin in meditation, 7) The Mass of St. Martin, 8) St. Martin and the emperor Valentinian, 9) The death of St. Martin, 10) Burial of the Saint.
On the wide span of the archway of the entrance to this chapel, on the left and begining at the top: St. Louis, king, St. Louis of Toulouse, St. Clare, St. Elizabeth of Hungary; on the left and begining at the top: St. Anthony of Padua and St. Francis, the Magdalen and St. Catherine of Alexandria.
Under the fascinating influence of the nearby frescoes painted by Giotto and his school, Martini blended together on the walls of this chapel the grace and delicacy of the gothic line beloved by the Sienese school and the pre-Renaissance Florentine worship of the human form and architectural composition. Here he achieved results rarely excelled by his other works, or by the painting of the Sienese school in general.
The stained glass of the three mullioned windows is probably the work of Giovanni di Bonino along lines similar to the work of Martini.

CENTRAL NAVE OF THE LOWER CHURCH. In this nave are found the oldest pictures in this Basilica. The frescoes are in bad condition, and they furthermore lack large portions. They had been cut away about the year 1270, when the large arches, made for the side chapels, were gradually added to the main body of the church.
The architectural style of the central nave and the short apse finds a pleasant counterbalance in the Gothic style of the adjoining chapels, which together with the large transept at the entrance were built after 1270. Actually the original plan of the church consisted only of the central nave and the two short transepts on the right and left of the high altar.

Chapel of St. Martin: *Episodes in St. Martin's life* by Simone Martini (1320)

Stained glass window in the chapel of St. Martin by Giovanni di Bonino (XIVth cent.)

Chapel of St. Martin: *St. Clare* (Simone Martini - 132(

Soon after the burial of St. Francis beneath the main altar of the church, the best artists were called to illustrate these walls and ceiling. The frescoes on the walls of the nave illustrate the parallelism in the life of Christ and Francis, his perfect follower. The same was done again later with regard to the nave's two transepts, and finally on the walls of the nave of the upper church. Those of the lower church were executed by an artist who had some affinity to Giunta Pisano, to whom for centuries the frescoes were attributed. By mutual agreement the critics called the unknown author: Maestro di San Francesco.

Maestro di S. Francesco *Crucifixion* (Detail)

Maestro di S. Francesco: *The sermon to the birds*

RIGHT SIDE

Looking toward the main altar begining on the right the following scenes were depicted: 1) Preparation for the Crucifixion, 2) The Crucifixion, 3) The Descent from the Cross, 4) Mourners at death of Christ, 5) Resurrection of Christ.

LEFT SIDE

Left side moving toward the altar: 1) St. Francis renounces material possessions, 2) Dream of Innocent III, 3) Sermon to the birds, 4) Stigmatization of St. Francis, 5) Burial of the Saint.

CHAPEL OF ST. LOUIS, KING, OR OF ST. STEPHEN. This is the first chapel on the right of the nave, and the one opposite the chapel of St. Martin. On the ceiling are depicted the four Prophets and the four Sybils; on the walls: St. Stephen in the synagogue and the martyrdom of St. Stephen, the work of Dono Doni about the year 1574.
The four stained glass windows of the large mullioned window containing figures of saints were presumably designed by Simone Martini.

CHAPEL OF ST. ANTHONY OF PADUA. Frescoes portraying the life of the Saint: His sermon before Gregory IX; Miracle of the Mule - they were done by Sermei and his pupil Martelli in 1610. The four mullioned stained glass windows portraying scenes from the life of the Saint were designed by a member of the school of Giotto in the fourteenth century (1300-1350).

Lower Basilica - Interior

CHAPEL OF ST. MARY MAGDALEN. This is the third and final chapel down at the right of the nave. Painted by Giotto about the year 1310, at the expenses of Teobaldo Pontano (d. 1329), bishop of Assisi. These frescoes were renewed or cleaned in 1967.

In the ceiling are bust figures of the Redeemer, Lazarus, Magdalen and Martha.

The frescoes on the walls are by Giotto and they portray the following scenes from the life of Mary Magdalen: on the left wall - 1) Dinner at the house of the Pharisee, 2) Resurrection of Lazarus; on the right wall: 3) Our Lord appears to Mary Magdalen after the Resurrection, 4) Mary Magdalen lands at Marseilles, 5) The Saint speaks with the angels. Above these frescoes: 6) Magdalen and the hermit Zosimo (on the wall of the entrance arch), 7) Com-

Chapel of St. Magdalen - GIOTTO - «*Noli me tangere*»

munion of M. Magdalen and the departure of her soul of Paradise (in the upper part of the left wall). On the arch of the entrance are paintings by Giotto of twelve saints. In the four stained glass windows are portrayed images of Christ, Mary Magdalen, Martha and Lazarus according to sketches of Florentine inspiration, but bearing a resemblance to The Roman school and done practically contemporaneously with the frescoes.

Chapel of St. Magdalen - GIOTTO: *St. Rufino and Teobaldo Pontano*

Chapel of St. Magdalen - GIOTTO: *The Resurrection of Lazarus*

CHAPEL OF ST. NICOLAS OF BARI. This chapel is situated in the apse of the right transept. It was built about 1270 by order of Cardinal Orsini (later Pope Nicolas III), and decorated at the expense of his nephews Napoleone and Cardinal Giangaetano Orsini (d. 1293), whose body lies buried behind the altar in a tomb sculptured by the school of Giovanni Cosma about 1310.

The frescoes were painted by an artist called the Master of St. Nicolas, assisted by Giotto, in the early decades of the fourteenth century. The excellent quality of the colors indicates Giotto as their author. Besides the numerous figures of the various saints in the lower area of the walls, beneath the entrance arch and in the lunette, there are nine panels containing the story of the life of St. Nicolas of Bari. On the underneath side of the great arch passing from top to bottom on the right: 1) St. Nicolas donates the dowry

to the three maidens, 2) Fresco destroyed, 3) The Saint blesses a penitent and other persons; (on the left) 4) The Saint saves three condemned persons, 5) Destroyed fresco, 6) The dream of Constantine; (on the right wall viewing from top downwards) 7) The Saint resuscitates a child, 8) Liberation of a slave, 9) The slave restored to his parents; (on the left wall from top downwards) 10) An old Hebrew attempts to destroy a marble bust of the Saint, 11) and 12) Destroyed frescoes. Above the tomb behind the altar are the Blessed Virgin Mary, St. Francis of Assisi and St. Nicolas.

The six windows in which are figured many saints and the two Orsini Brothers and their coat of arms, were executed before 1342 from the design of the same artists of the frescoes.

Lower Basilica: Right Transept: GIOTTO: *Crucifixion*

RIGHT TRANSEPT OF THE MAIN ALTAR. These paintings were restored in 1968. On the wall of the arched entrance to the chapel of St. Nicolas is the Annunciation. In the ceiling: The Visitation, The Nativity, The adoration by the Magi, The Presentation, The Crucifixion. On the opposite side of the vaulted ceiling: The Flight into Egypt, The Slaughter of the Innocents, The Boy Jesus in the Temple of Jerusalem, The Return of the Holy Family to Nazareth. All these paintings are the work of Giotto and his pupils working under the direction of their master about the year 1315.

On the wall near the choir, St. Francis resuscitates a child which had fallen from the house; on the wall of the arched access to the chapel of St. Nicolas another miracle is portrayed: the resuscitation of a child which had been killed by the collapse of the house. On the right wall of the arched access from left to right: St. Francis, St. Louis of Toulouse,

Lower Basilica: Right Transept: GIOTTO: *Nativity*

Lower Basilica: Right Transept: GIOTTO: *Presentation in the temple*

St. Elizabeth of Hungary (?), St. Clare (?), and an unknown saint. All these paintings are the work of Simone Martini. Near the door of access to the side chapel of Mary Magdalen, the Madonna wearing a crown, St. Elizabeth and St. Louis IX of France: the work of Simone Martini. To the right of this same portal: Blessed John the Englishman (fifteenth century), and above the iron grill where the bodies of five companions of St. Francis lie buried, their images. These five portraits are by Pietro Lorenzetti.

Lower Basilica: Right Transept: GIOTTO: *Adoration of the Magi*

The Madonna enthroned with the Child Jesus, the Angels and St. Francis, a painting by Cimabue (c. 1280?). Ruskin describes this as the most noble Sorrowful Mother of all christian art. The portrait of St. Francis corresponds closely to the description of him given by his first biographer, Fra Tommaso da Celano. The color has become obscure and has taken on a languid yellow rose tone. The solemnity and the depth of this work is superceded by the great work influenced by Cimabue in the upper church.

Lower Basilica: Right Transept: GIOTTO: *Flight into Egypt*

Lower Basilica: Right Transept: SIMONE MARTINI: *St. Clare*

Lower Basilica: Right Transept: SIMONE MARTINI: *St. Francis*

VAULT OF THE MAIN ALTAR AND CHOIR. Immediately before arriving at the main altar at the left we find a tribune done by an anonymous sculptor who worked between 1250 and 1300. On the wall is the Coronation of Our Lady by Puccio Capanna of Assisi, middle of the fourteenth century. Underneath the same arch, the Martyrdom of St. Stanislaus, and St. Stanislaus restores a dead man to life (by Puccio Capanna), and finally the Crucifixion (done in collaboration with the same artist).

Lower Basilica: *Main Altar*

The main altar itself is a work done by an anonymous Cosmatesque about 1250. It contains twenty small columns ornamented by mosaics. The mensa or altar table consists of a marble monolith which is thought to have come from Constantinople.
The frescoes above the ceiling vault, restored in 1968, examined very carefully, are ascribed to Giotto and his school (1315-1320). As works of art they are of excellent quality in technique and color, beyond their theological content. Tradition has it that the allegorical concepts were given to Giotto by a theologian, perhaps Jacopone da Todi, an artist endowed with a sensitive if not figurative imagination. The formation of the area poorly suited to the horizontal development of the giottesque scenographic compositions, made it necessary to paint slender figures and to reduce the design. Those who ordered the work to be done had asked for a rather complex, richly and detailed elaborated painting.

ɔwer Basilica: Right Transept: CIMABUE: *St. Francis* (Detail)

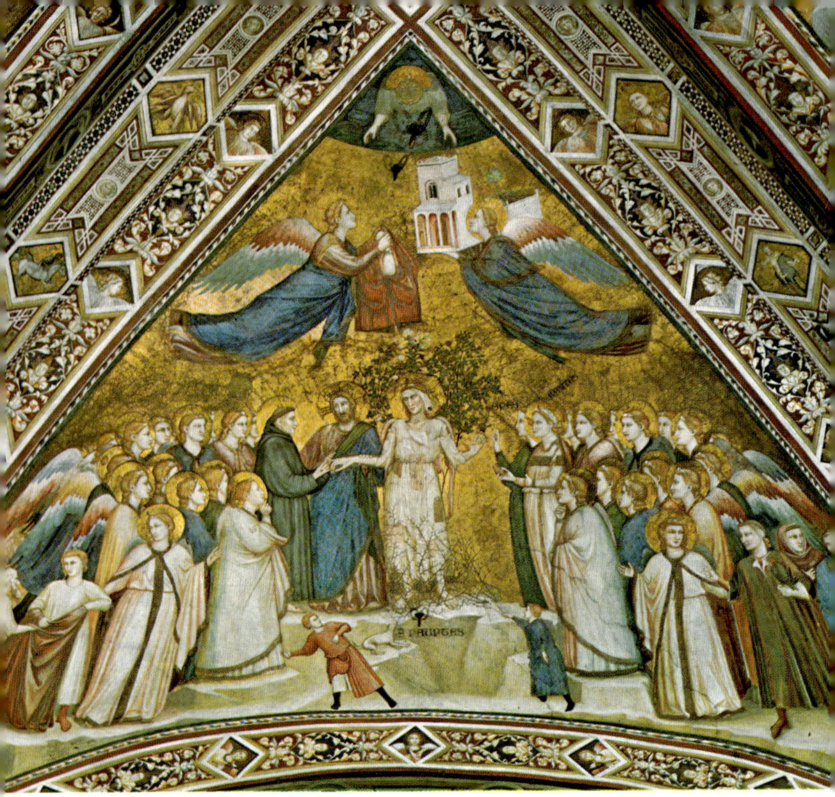

Allegory of Poverty

ALLEGORY OF POVERTY. At the center of this painting we see the mystical marriage of Francis to Lady Poverty. They are blessed by Christ and are surrounded by a beautiful throng of angels.

In the lower left corner of the painting is a young man in the act of offering his mantle to a poor person. He is invited by an angel to look upon Lady Poverty, and espouse her, as Francis had done. In the lower right corner an angel invites well-to-do persons to do likewise, but scoffing at the invitation, they clutch their treasure to their bosom.

At the bottom in the center boys and animals attack Lady Poverty; one tosses a stone at her, while the dog barks, and the other holds a stick by means of which he is pushing thorns against the bare feet of Lady Poverty. But miraculously the thorns grow and are changed into a garland of roses about the head of Lady Poverty. In the very peak of the painting, the Eternal Father accepts as gifts given to Him the offerings made to the poor in His name.

Allegory of Chastity

ALLEGORY OF CHASTITY. Chastity is symbolized by a maiden clothed in white, having her hands joined in prayer. She is enclosed in a castle above which flutters a white banner. Two angels in flight bring the maiden the palm and diadem of victory. Soldiers guard the castle; from the inside above the wall two figures, Holy Purity and Holy Fortitude, are handing a shield and a banner to a youth, who is submitting himself to a birth of regeneration.
In the left corner St. Francis assists three persons to be received into his knightly and religious Order: they stand for the three Franciscan Orders which are represented by Fra Giovanni da Muro, St. Clare (II Order), and Dante Alighieri (III Order).
In the right corner, the three crowned virtues assisted solely by Holy Penance (the curved hooded figure), put to flight impurity, death and immodesty.

Allegory of Obedience

ALLEGORY OF OBEDIENCE. Holy Obedience is represented by a winged monastic figure seated in the center of a loggia. With one hand this figure enjoins silence, with the other it places a yoke upon the kneeling friar. The features of Obedience are both beautiful and serene. Two virtues are assisting Obedience: on the left Holy Prudence with its two faces, and on the right the charming countenance of Holy Humility. Just below Prudence we find a kneeling angel who is presenting two devout persons (perhaps those who ordered the fresco); beneath Humility there is another keeling angel who is restraining from coming forward a centaur which represents Pride.
On high in the peak of the triangle and between two angels stands St. Francis, girded with a yoke and guided by two hands descending from heaven.

St. Francis in Glory

ST. FRANCIS IN GLORY. Surrounded by a festive choir of dancing and singing angels, Francis is seated upon a throne with a brocade canopy; he is robed in a white dalmatic interwoven with gold. He holds a Cross and the Book of the Gospels in his stigmatized hands.

Having effectively made use of his poverty, chastity and obedience as a means to be free to bring God's love to man, Francis finally found his «perfect joy». «Francis poor and humble enters heaven rich; he is honored with heavenly hymns. Alleluia». (Mass in honor of St. Francis, Oct. 4).

THE CHOIR. The choir stalls were carved by Apollonio da Ripatransone and his associates in 1471. There are fifty choir stalls arranged in two tiers, each stall having arm rests ornamented with leaves, figures of animals and of men. The back rest have inlaid designs by Florentine artists. The design was conceived by Paolino di Mastro Giovanni da Ascoli, who began the work in 1467.

On the choir vault is a scene portraying the Last Judgement by Cesare Sermei done about 1623. In order to provide a place for this painting of mediocre value, a fresco by Puccio Capanna was destroyed. The windows are of recent date and they portray, from left to right, St. Clare, St. Francis and St. Elizabeth (Lodovico, Rosa and Cecilia Caselli, 1921-1924).

LEFT TRANSEPT OF THE MAIN ALTAR. Pietro Lorenzetti is held to be the author of these frescoes, done about 1320. On the ceiling and walls is the series depicting Our Lord's Passion and Glorification (restored in 1963): Entrance into Jerusalem, The Last Supper, The Washing of the Feet, Capture of Jesus in the Garden of Gethsemane. From the uppermost part of the arched ceiling in the opposite direction: The Flagellation, The Way to Calvary, and the (grandiose) Crucifixion. Beneath is the well-known Madonna with Bambino, St. Francis and St. John the Evangelist, traditionally called the the Madonna of the Sunset. On the left wall to the left of the archway of access to the chapel of St. John the Baptist is the scene of the Descent into Limbo (upper part), and the Descent from the Cross (lower part). Below, from left to right, are four half figures of saints: St. Nicolas, St. Catherine, St. Clare, St. Tecla. On the right wall of the archway is the Resurrection (above), and below is the Sepulchre. Directly above the stairs at the left is the Hanging of Judas, while at the right is the Stigmata of St. Francis.

CHAPEL OF ST. JOHN THE BAPTIST. This chapel is located in the apse of this left transept. Above the altar, the Blessed Virgin, St. Francis, and St. John the Baptist by Peter Lorenzetti. In the central mullioned window are figures of saints and ornaments, designed by Maestro di San Francesco or by Cimabue. The side mullioned windows are the work of S. Feliciano di Foligno in the fifteenth century, except for the saint up on high on the left by Cimabue, and the other portions up higher recently restored by Pennacchi.

Lower Basilica: Left Transept: P. LORENZETTI (1330): *Crucifixion and Descent from the Cross*

Lower Basilica: Left Transept: P. LORENZETTI: *Stigmata of St. Francis and Madonna of the Sunset*

Lower Basilica: Left Transept: P. LORENZETTI: *Resurrection*

CHAPEL OF THE RELICS - CHAPTER HALL

In 1982, on the occasion of the eighth centenary of the birth of St. Francis, precious relics of the Saint had been relocated to this chapel which dates back to the thirteenth century and in which is found a

beautiful painting of the crucifixion by PUCCIO CAPANNA. Venerated in this chapel are: the *tunuic and capuche worn* by St. Francis; a *hairshirt* used by him for penance, *sandals* made by St. Clare and worn by St. Francis when he was sick; a piece of *chamois leather* from the wound of the stigmata on the Saint's side; a *white tunic* worn by St. Francis during the last year of his life; *linen cloths* (a gift from "Friar" Jacopa dei Settesoli, a noble lady of Rome) used to wipe the brow of the Saint in his last agony; a *chalice* used by St. Francis, when, as a deacon, he assisted in the celebration of the eucharistic liturgy; an *ivory horn* given to the Saint by the Sultan of Egypt, Malek el Kamel.
Beacause of their spiritual and historical significance, two relics are most precious: the *Franciscan Rule* of 1223, approved by Pope Honorius III, considered the Magna Charta of the Franciscan movement, and the *Blessing* given to *Brother leo* in the Saint's own handwriting.

The grey tunic of St. Francis

These mementos give witness to the manifold mission of St. Francis: the *Rule* attest to his life in the community of his brothers; the *gray tunic* to his place in the society of his day; the *sandals* to his life as an itinerant preacher; and the *ivory horn* to his ecumenical spirit.

Autographed Blessing of St. Francis to Brother Leo

Since liturgical functions are frequently celebrated in this chapel, visits are restricted to certain hours. To visit the chapel of the relics, please make arrangements with one of the Friars of the Basilica.

Cloister of Sixtus IV: *Apse*

CLOISTER OF SIXTUS IV. Access to the upper church is via two stairways built into the wall of the two cross transepts. The cloister of Sixtus IV is so named after the Pope who had the upper loggia built by Gasparino da Lugano. The lower cloister around which arose the original convent built by Brother Elias was given its present arrangement a few decades before Sixtus IV. Along the walls of the two-storied loggia are fragments of frescoes of the life of St. Francis by Dono Doni (c. 1574).

Aerial view of the Basilica St. Francis

VISIT TO THE BASILICA: UPPER CHURCH

HARMONY OF ART AND FAITH

The silence, austerity and somberness of the lower church symbolizes the humanity and humility of the Poverello, and reminds us of the sad portions of our own life, while at the same time inviting us to mystical contemplation, prayer, and to the search of the true good, the peace and joy of spirit which Francis wished for all. In contrast to the lower church, the upper is high vaulted, airy, naturally well illuminated by its spacious windows. In this way it symbolizes the sanctity and glory of Francis, while opening our heart to the hope of eternal happiness.
The Gothic of the upper church has an Italian touch: to the elegance, harmony, rhythm and balance is added a tone of delicacy, calm and serenity distinctively Italian, Umbrian and Franciscan. It is an authentic art because it is a perfectly harmonious encounter of splendor, religiousness and art.
Having completed the finishing touches (1270-1280) the Friars entrusted the decoration of the cross transept to Cimabue who painted here between 1280-1283. In the left transept there are scenes from the Apocalypse and a Crucifixion, while in the right

one are the Acts of the Apostles and a Crucifixion. In the ceiling vault above the main altar are the allegories of the four Evangelists. Almost representations on the first two sections of the nave various painters of a Roman school made frescoes on the vault and the upper areas of the walls depicting stories of the Old and New Testament. These frescoes have been ascribed to various authors — among others to Torriti, Cavallini, Rusuti, Giotto, and Cimabue. From what remains of these frescoes it seems quite certain that this judgement can be made: there is a notable influence of Cimabue upon these Roman painters of the biblical scenes in the upper zones of the walls of the nave. Furthermore it is difficult to deny some influence of Giotto upon part of the frescoes of the third section, and upon all or almost all of the fourth section.
One or two years later, or contemporaneously with the frescoes of the fourth section, between 1296-1298, Giotto began to paint along the lower part of the wall of the nave the Leggenda di S. Francesco. These twenty eight paintings of Assisi bring to a close the pictorial Italian thirteenth century. In the multi-centuried development of art they constitute a milestone, because they belong to the past by being its termination, culmination and recapitulation; at the same time they belong to the future by being its foundation and by leveling the way for modern art. If, in the painters of the upper Basilica, one senses a gradual separation, a progressive differentiation from the medieval vision of nature and from the Byzantine forms and stylized Romanesque and Gothic currents, all this does not signify negation or refusal. It signifies rather a fusion of values which glitter separately in the various currents of the previous Middle Ages.

2. TRANSEPTS AND CHOIR

RIGHT TRANSEPT. Only the lower section was painted by Cimabue (1280-1283). The frescoes are in bad condition. From left to right scenes from the Acts of the Apostles: The healing of the paralytic, The cure of many sick people, The fall of Simon Magus, Crucifixion of St. Peter, The beheading of St. Paul. In the lower section behind the small altar is the Crucifixion.

Upper Basilica: CIMABUE: *Crucifixion*

In the lunette of the upper section: The Transfiguration, and on the opposite wall Christ in Glory. In the rest of the sections figures of angels, apostles, and various ornamental designs. The frescoes in the upper zone of the transept, different in their dominant tonality of color from the others in this transept, are the work of an unknown English painter who preceded Cimabue.

The four mullioned windows are the work of a master of the Roman school about the end of the thirteenth century. The work shows Byzantine influence together with definite Romanic characteristics. In the left mullioned window are geometric motifs; in the right one are figurations from the Old and New Testament.

THE APSE. The apse was painted by Cimabue (1280-1283). The paintings are in a poor state of preservation. They depicted scenes from the life of the Blessed Virgin in the following order: Annunciation to Joachim (upper left wall), Nativity of the Virgin Mary (upper right wall), Presentation of Mary in the Temple (below the first), Betrothal of the Blessed Virgin Mary (below the second); in the lower zone to the right — The virgin Mary dying, The death of Mary, The Assumption, The Glorification of Mary. All the remaining area was painted by Cimabue.
The three mullioned windows are the work of anonymous artists of a German school done toward the end of the thirteenth century. These show possibly the influence of some skilled French glasswindow artist, especially in the left mullioned window. The scenes on the left refer to the life of Christ; those on the right portray the Old Testament.

THE CHOIR. The wooden choir stalls are the work of Domenico di Antonio Indivini from S. Severino and his assistants (1491-1501), ordered by the Minister General of the Conventuals, P. Sansone. There are one hundred choir stalls carved and inlaid according to designs of the Marches under the influence of Crivelli. In the thirty eight panels of the upper stalls are inlaid figures of the Annunciation (both sides), and of Franciscans famous for their sanctity, learning and apostolate. In the lower panels are geometric and floral designs. The choir stalls conceal the recently installed pipes of the organ.
The wooden reading stand was done by the same artist, Indivini (1501).
We also find a Papal Throne (c. 1250) composed of disparate elements from different places.

LEFT TRANSEPT. The paintings are by Cimabue (1280-1283) and depict scenes from the Apocalypse: Upper right wall - St. Michael casts Lucifer out of Paradise; lower section of wall from left to right: St. John the Evangelist on Patmos, Destruction of Babylon, Coming of Christ in Judgement, Angels of the Apocalypse, Mystical Lamb. In back of the small altar is the majestic Crucifixion (Cimabue).
The union of the chromatic monotony, the result of the oxidization of the lead in the whites, with the plasticity of the figures (you can almost, as it were, reach out and touch them), causes a dramatic effect

Upper Basilica: *The wooden choir stalls of Domenico Indovini* (1491-1501)

Upper Basilica: GIOTTO: *Nativity and Betrayal by Judas*

in which we easily perceive the grief of the pious women, and the hatred of the executioners.
The four mullioned stained glass window are probably the work of an anonymous French master toward the end of the thirteenth century, as may be inferred from the intimate exquisiteness and linearity of adornment, and from the refined and minute polycromy evident in the work.

Upper Basilica: Anonymous French Master: Four stained glass windows

The pulpit to the left of the altar was done perhaps by Niccolò da Bettona (1330-1347). It is a not too successful imitation of other fourteenth century masterpieces.
The main altar is the work of a Cosmatesco contemporaneous with the consecration of the church (1253).

THE NAVE. There are in all thirty-four frescoes in the upper and middle sections, and twenty eight in the lower sections.

Upper Basilica: GIOTTO: *Deception by Jacob*

RIGHT WALL, ON THE UPPER PART. This will be on the left as you stand with your back to the Papal Throne. Begining from left to right: Creation of the World, Creation of Adam, Creation of Eve, Original Sin, fresco destroyed (perhaps the sacrifice of Cain of Abel), Fragment (murder of Abel?). All by the Roman school.
In the lower register, from left to right: Building of the Ark (Roman school, XIII century), Entrance of the animals into the Ark (Roman school, XIII century), Sacrifice of Isaac (Roman school), Visit of the angels to Abraham (Roman school), Visit of the angels to Abraham (Roman school), Deception by Jacob (perhaps by Giotto c. 1290-1295), Esau reclaims his birthright (Giotto), Joseph sold by his brothers (Giotto), Brothers of Joseph in Egypt (Giotto).

LEFT WALL, ON THE UPPER PART. Annunciation (Roman school, influence of Cimabue), Fragments of the Visitation (unknown author), The Nativity (Roman school), Adoration by the Magi (Roman school, influence of Cimabue), Presentation of Jesus in the Temple (Roman school), Flight into

Upper Basilica: GIOTTO: *Four Doctors of the Church*

Egypt — traces (Roman school), Dispute in the Temple (Roman school), Baptism of Jesus (Roman school).
In the lower register: Wedding at Cana (Roman school, influence of Cimabue c. 1290-1295), Resurrection of Lazarus (?) — traces (Roman school), Capture in the Garden (Roman school), Christ before Pilate (?) — fragments, Way to Calvary (Giotto 1290-1295) Crucifixion (Giotto assisted by Duccio), Burial of Christ (Giotto), Women at the sepulchre (Giotto).

REAR WALL. On the right is the Ascension (Giotto); while on the left the Pentecost (Giotto). On the entrance portal Madonna with child (by Giotto after 1296); in the underside of the arch connecting the section to the end wall are sixteen figures of saints (influence of Giotto, end of the thirteenth century).
Holy Water Font: work done at end of the thirteenth century.
Ceiling vault, fourth section: Four Doctors of the Church (influence of Giotto 1295-1296). Second section: The Virgin, The Redeemer, John the Baptist, St. Francis (by Turriti c. 1290).

Upper Basilica: GIOTTO: *St. Augustine Doctor*

STAINED GLASS WINDOWS. Looking toward the altar on the right: the first and second mullioned window, not having any figures in relief, and given the rhythmic thrust of lines in the folds, the contours of the figures and the architecture of the totality, reveal a French authorship of the end of the thirteenth century (design by the master of St. Francis). The Byzantine-like characters in the third window and the robustness of the design in the fourth window indicate they are of the Roman school of the end of the thirteenth century (design by the Master of St. Francis).

With regard to the windows on the left side, the first and second by reason of their characters, are closely associated with the two preceding of the Roman school at the end of the thirteenth century; the third and fourth windows with figures of the Apostles and decorative designs are partly ancient (end of the thirteenth century) like those in front, and partly modern.

Upper Basilica: Stained glass windows: *Stigmata of St. Francis*

GIOTTO (1296-1300)

LOWER SECTION OF THE WALLS. These twenty eight frescoes depict scenes from the life of St. Francis, by Giotto (1296-1300). The narrative begins on the right wall (looking toward the main altar). Beneath each fresco runs a Latin text describing the fresco which was reconstructed by the Franciscan Father Marinangeli and is repeated in this guide book.

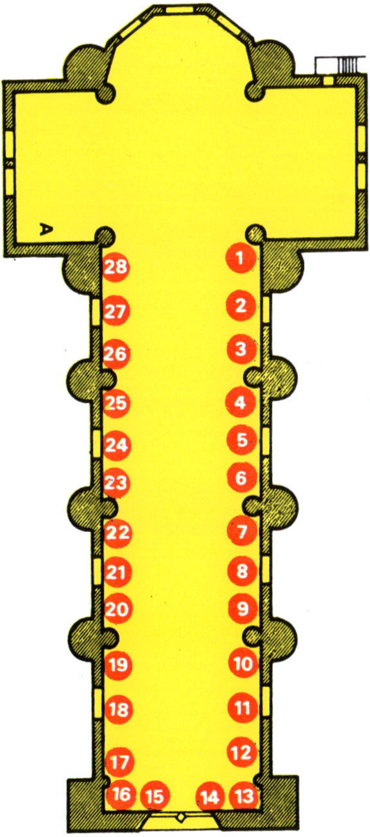

Upper Basilica Plan

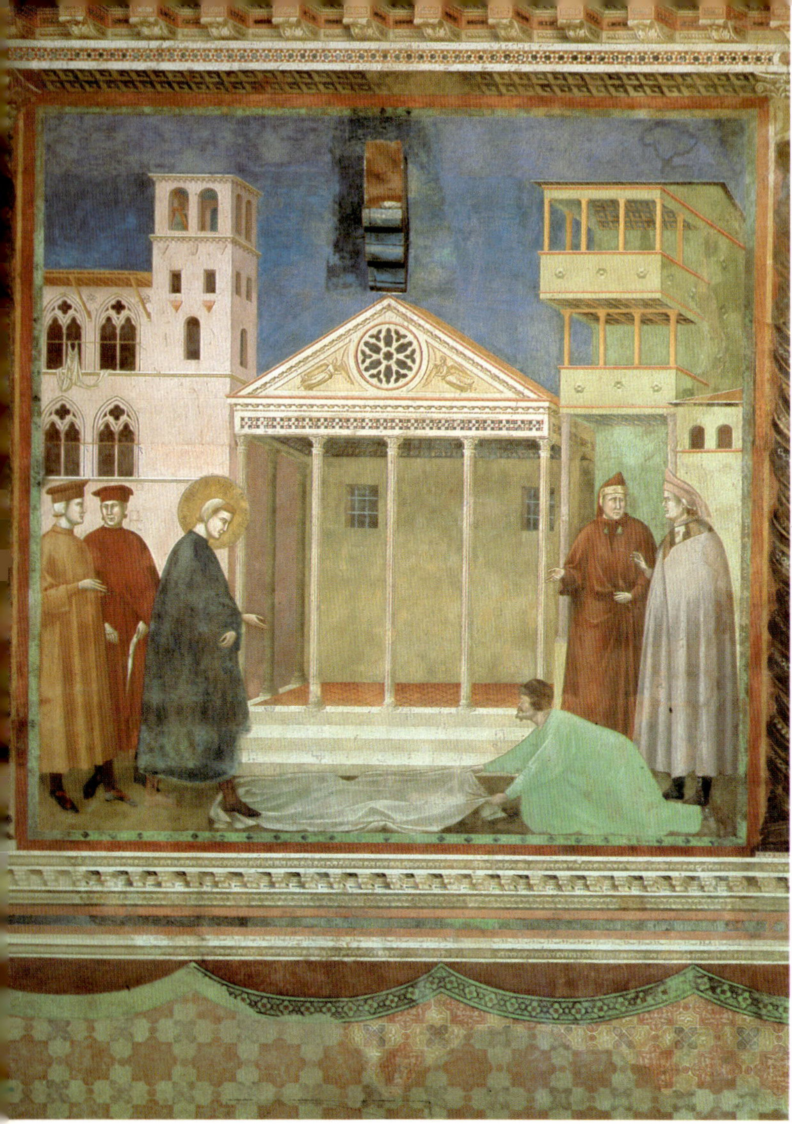

1. FRANCIS HONORED BY A FELLOW CITIZEN. *This fresco shows an ordinary citizen of Assisi spreading his cloak on the ground before Francis, then still a youth; thus he gave honor to Francis and asserted, one may believe, under inspiration from God, that Francis was worthy of respect and reverence by all because he was going to accomplish great things.*

2. FRANCIS GIVES AWAY HIS CLOAK. *When Francis chanced to meet a nobleman, destitute and poorly clothed, he was moved by compassion and immediately doffed his cloak and gave it to the man.*

3. THE DREAM OF THE PALACE FILLED WITH WEAPONS. *Francis had a dream one night in which he saw a splendid and sumptuous palace equipped with knightly armament, and with weapons embellished with the sign of the Cross of Christ. When Francis asked to whom all this belonged, he received the reply from on high: that it would all belong to him and his knights.*

4. FRANCIS BEFORE THE CRUCIFIX AT SAN DAMIANO. *When Francis was praying one day before the image of the Crucified Savior, a voice from the image spoke to him and said three times: «Francis go and repair my house which is falling completely into ruin», signifying the Roman Church.*

5. RENUNCIATION OF HIS INHERITANCE AND EARTHLY POSSESSIONS. *Francis gave back everything to his father even the clothes he was wearing, renounced his right of inheritance and said to his father: «Henceforth with all certainty I can say Our Father who art in heaven because Peter Bernardone has repudiated me».*

6. THE DREAM OF POPE INNOCENT III. *The Pope in a dream saw the Lateran Basilica about to collapse but a little poor man, Francis of Assisi, put his shoulders to the building and prevented it from falling into ruin.*

7. THE APPROVAL OF THE RULE. *Pope Innocent III approved the Rule of Francis and gave the friars the mission to preach penance, and to the friars who had accompanied Francis, the Pope granted permission to wear the tonsure so that they might preach the divine word.*

8. THE VISION OF THE FIERY CHARIOT. *One day Francis was praying in a hovel (near the Bishop's residence in Assisi). His friars who were then in Rivotorto, quite a distance away, saw Francis in a bright fiery chariot moving around in the place about midnight. The place was illuminated as bright as day to the fear and amazement of the friars who were awake at the time, and of the others who were awakened to see this spectacle.*

9. THE VISION OF THE THRONES IN HEAVEN.

In a vision a friar saw many thrones in heaven, one among which was more glorious and resplendent than the others. He heard a voice which said: «This throne belonged to one of the angels cast out of paradise; now it is reserved for the humble Francis».

10. THE DEMONS CAST OUT OF AREZZO. *Seeing above the city of Arezzo many triumphant demons, Francis said to his campanion Father Silvester: «Go, and in the name of God cast out the demons... shouting at the gate». Obeying the command, Silvester shouted and the demons fled. Peace was immediately restored.*

11. THE CHALLENGE BEFORE THE SULTAN.
In testimony to the truth of the faith of Christ, Francis challenged the priests of the Sultan of Babylonia to walk through fire with him. But none of them was willing to accept the challenge; they all fled immediately from the presence of Francis and the Sultan.

12. ECSTASY OF FRANCIS. *One day as Francis was wrapt in fervent prayer, the friars saw him raised above the ground, with his arms extended heavenward. A bright cloud surrounded him.*

13. THE CRIB AT GRECCIO. *In memory of the birth of Christ at Bethlehem, Francis wanted to reproduce the scene. He asked that a crib be prepared, straw fetched, an an ox and ass be brought to the crib. He then gave a sermon about the birth of the poor King; while he was in prayer, a knight present for this ceremony saw the Infant Jesus come take the place of the baby Francis had placed in the crib.*

14. MIRACLE OF THE FOUNTAIN. *Ascending a mountain on the back of a donkey of a certain poor man — since Francis was ailing — Francis prayed and caused water to come forth from a rock in order to quench the thirst of this suffering poor man.*

15. SERMON TO THE BIRDS. *Going one day to the town of Bevagna, Francis preached to a flock of birds which expressed their joy by flapping their wings, extending their heads forward, opening their beaks and even touching his tunic. The friars who were awaiting at the roadside witnessed this scene.*

16. DEATH OF THE KNIGHT OF CELANO. *A nobleman of Celano invited Francis to dinner. Francis implored God the grace of salvation for his host. The man made his confession, later put his affairs in order, and while the others were at table, he suddenly died in the Lord.*

17. SERMON IN THE PRESENCE OF HONORIUS III. *Francis preached so devoutly and so efficaciously before the Pope and the Cardinals that it was clear to all that he did not speak with the learned words of human wisdom but by divine inspiration.*

18. APPARITION AT THE CHAPTER OF ARLES. *While St. Anthony of Padua was preaching about the Cross, at the Chapter of Arles, Francis appeared, extended his hands and blessed the friars. A certain Monaldo saw this. The friars rejoiced immensely.*

19. STIGMATIZATION OF FRANCIS. *Praying one day on the slope of Mount Verna, Francis saw Christ in the form of a crucified seraph which imprinted in his hands and feet and right side the sacred stigmata of our Lord and Saviour Jesus Christ.*

20. THE DEATH OF FRANCIS. *In the moment of the death of Francis, a friar beheld the soul of the Saint ascending to heaven in the form of a brilliant star.*

21. THE APPARITION TO BROTHER AUGUSTINE AND TO THE BISHOP OF ASSISI.
At the very moment when Francis died, Brother Augustine, Minister in southern Italy, sick and near death, deprived of speech, suddenly cried out: «Wait for me, Father Francis, I'm coming with you», whereupon he died and followed his seraphic Father. The Bishop of Assisi, at the time at Monte S. Angelo in southern Italy, saw the Blessed Francis who said to him: «I'm going to heaven».

22. CERTIFICATION OF THE STIGMATA. *While the mortal remains of Francis lay at the Porziuncola, Doctor Geronimo, a famous doctor and scholar touched the nail marks, and examined the wounds in the hands, feet and side of the body of Francis.*

23. THE GRIEF OF THE POOR CLARES. *The crowd which had assembled, carrying branches and lighted candles, transported the sacred body, adorned with the stigmata, towards Assisi. At San Damiano the procession halted so that Clare and her sisters might see the sacred remains.*

24. THE CANONIZATION OF ST. FRANCIS. *Pope Gregory IX came personally to Assisi, and after the miracles had been duly examined, on the basis of the testimony of the friars, canonized Francis and enrolled him in the calendar of the saints.*

25. APPARITION TO GREGORY IX. *When Pope Gregory was somewhat in doubt about the wound in the side of Francis, the latter appeared to him in a dream and said: «Give me an empty vial». This he took and filled it with blood that came forth from the wound in his side.*

26. INSTANTANEOUS CURE OF A PERSON DEVOTED TO ST. FRANCIS. *St. Francis undid the bandages and delicately touched the wounds of Giovanni di Ylerda who was deathly ill, for whom the physicians entertained no hope; but the sick man had prayed to Francis and received a miraculous cure.*

27. CONFESSION OF A WOMAN RESTORED TO LIFE. *This deceased woman had died with an unconfessed sin on her soul. St. Francis restored her to life. In the presence of the clergy and others she went to confession, and thereafter died peacefully in the Lord, to the confusion of the devil.*

28. LIBERATION OF THE PENITENT HERETIC.

St. Francis liberated this prisoner, accused of heresy, and by order of the Pope placed under the authority of the Bishop of Tivoli. This happened on the feast of St. Francis. According to custom, the accused man had fasted on the vigil of the feast.

MUSEUM

The art museum, relocated in the Cloister of Sixtus IV, was opened on October 4, 1977. The exhibits, from the XII to XVIII cent., offer witness to the vitality of religious life at this Franciscan Shrine, and point to the consequences of numerous wars which despoiled the church of its treasures.
The exhibits include: *Madonna and Child* in wood; *a processional cross «vivus et triumphans»* (XII cent.); a fragment of a polyptych of the *prophet Isaiah* by the Master of St. Francis; a crucifix by the «Master of the Blue Cross»; a painting of *St. Francis with four miracles* wrought after his death, a synopia from the upper church by a Roman Master; a *Madonna and Child* by the French school; *the missal of St. Louis; a synopia of St. Martin* giving his cloak to a poor man; a *chalice* of Nicholas IV (XIII cent.); *altar* frontal of Sixtus IV; *a Flemish* tapestry depicting the glory of the Franciscan Order.

THE PERKINS COLLECTION. The art critic, Frederick Mason Perkins (1874-1955), donated 57 art pieces from his private collection to the Sacro Convento in apprecition to Italy and to Assisi (he was baptized a Catholic and took the name Francis). These comprise the works of major and minor artists (XIV-XVI cent.) of the schools of Florence, Siena, and Venice, such as Pietro Lorenzetti, Fra Angelico, Signorelli, Bartolomeo della Gatta, Pier Francesco Fiorentino, il "Sassetta", Sebastian Marinaredi, Sano di Pietro, John di Paolo, Lorenzo Monaco, Masolino Panicale, Taddeo di Bartolo and others.

Museum of the Basilica:
Maestro di S. Francesco:
Crucifixion

Museum of the Basilica:
Bonaventura Berlinghieri:
St. Francis (XIIIth cent.)

CITY OF ASSISI AND SURROUNDINGS

FROM ST. FRANCIS BASILICA TO THE PIAZZA DEL COMUNE. Standing on the large piazza before the Upper Church one has a view of the plain, the Valley of Spoleto. Francis himself said he had never seen any place more beautiful than this valley. The populated area in the valley below Assisi is S. Maria degli Angeli with its magnificent church dominated by the beautiful dome which guards the chapel of the Porziuncola. Off to the left, some distance away, is the Sanctuary of Rivotorto which houses the stable that served as the first friary of Francis and his brethren. He moved from this location to locate definitely at the Porziuncola.
Standing in front of the Basilica of St. Francis, looking toward the city, one sees off to the left the Porta S. Giacomo, and high above the look-out tower of the Fortress of Assisi.
Before going to the Piazza del Commune, by walking to the left and following the first street skirting the grassy piazza, the Via Merry del Val, one comes to the Porta San Giacomo constructed in the twelfth century and restored by Albornoz, (about 1365). On

Panorama of Assisi

top of the gate notice the centuries old cypress. Passing through the portal one comes upon a very beautiful view of the hills and the picturesque valley of the Tescio.
Retracing one's steps back through the portal or gate, and ascending the street about two hundred meters one comes to the Church of San Giacomo de Muro Rupto. This church, constructed in 1088, is Romanesque in style and has one nave, the walls of which are of bare stone with some fragments of frescoes dating from the fifteenth century. Part remains of the ancient cloister with two arched mullioned windows and the well.
After returning to the piazza of the Basilica, one may set forth on the Via S. Francesco, the most important arterial street of Assisi.
At the right at no. 19 is the Palazzo Barnabei, formerly Sperelli, begun according to the design made by Giacomo Giorgetti of Assisi in the seventeenth century. It was never completed.
Further down on the left at no. 14 is the house of the Comacini Masters with the coat of arms of this cor-

poration sculptured in stone, a work dating from 1474. It is a building in thirteenth century style, remodelled in the fifteenth century, and still later with the erection of the tower.
A short distance farther down one comes upon the Oratory dei Pellegrini which was originally a part of the no longer existing Ospedale dei Pellegrini. Beneath the large extending roof is a rather badly damaged fresco of Pier Antonio Mezzastris (fifteenth century) portraying Our Redeemer in glory amid a throng of angels, saints, and the two titular saints: Anthony the Abbot and James.
The interior of this oratory is ornamented with precious frescoes of the fifteenth century by the Umbrian school. On the back wall The Blessed Virgin Mary with the Christ Child amid angel musicians, St. James and St. Anthony, Abbot. To the left an angel and a scroll bearing the date 1468 and the signature of the painter Matteo da Gualdo. Up above the Annunciation.
On the right wall two scenes of a miracle performed by St. James.
On the left wall two episodes in the life of St. Anthony, Abbott: he preaches to and blesses the camels; he gives alms to the poor.
Following the street again at no. 8 is the sixteenth century Palazzo Bartocci, formerly Bindagoli, erected by the Perugian Giulio Danti on previously existing costruction dating from the thirteenth century.
The fountain bears the name Fonte Oliviera and dates from the sixteenth century.
Just beyond the Seminary Arch which formed part of the ancient city boundary, on the right is the Diocesan Seminary, built in the fourteenth century and reconstructed in the sixteenth, which embodies also the ancient monastery of St. Angelo in Panzo.
A few meters farther along an arrow on the left indicates the way to the little church of St. Stephen, constructed in the twelfth but remodelled in the thirteenth century. The interior is graceful with its five sections and semicircular apse. It is the seat of the St. Stephen Confraternity which left us a canticle of praise in the vernacular (fourteenth century). Tradition has it that the bells of this church miraculously began to toll while St. Francis was dying.
Returning to the Via del Seminario one enters the little Piazza Garibaldi; thence one may descend to the Via A. Cristofani to the Oratory of St. Leonard call-

ed S. Francescuccio, mention of which is made in documents already in 1217. On the façade is a fresco entitled Le Opere di Misericordia (of the latter part of the fifteenth century, a one color fresco in green). In the niche of the door scenes from the Istitution of the Porziuncola Indulgence (from the second half of the fifteenth century).

In the interior behind the altar the Crucifixion, painted by Giovanni di Corraduccio (end of the fourteenth century).

Entering from the Via Giotto one proceeds to the begining of the Via Portica. At about the top of the ascent on the left is the Museum and the Foro Romano. The entrance area, in which there are urns, Etruscan pillars, Roman statues is all that remains of the Crypt of the Church of St. Nicolas (of the eleventh century).

Church of St. Stephen

PIAZZA DEL COMUNE. On the left the Temple of Minerva (first century before Christ), now dedicated to the Madonna. Adjacent is the tower of the Municipality (Torre Comunale built between 1275 and 1305. At the base of the tower are the standard measures of the Municipality in use up to the end of the thirteenth century. Farther to the left, the Palazzo del Capitano del Popolo, built between 1212 and 1282. On the right hand side of the piazza: the Palazzo dei Priori (begun in 1337), the seat of the municipal administration and of the Pinacoteca Civica containing paintings of the Umbrian school from the twelfth to the seventeenth century.
Following along the Corso Mazzini on the right is an archway surmounted by a graceful polycrome ceramic which bears the invitation to descend the short stairway to visit the Oratorio di S. Francesco Piccolino where the Saint was born.

SAN FRANCESCO PICCOLINO. This is the sacred spot where the Saint was born. Shortly after 1250, Piccardo, the son of Angelo and nephew of the Saint, turned this storage-place room of the house of St. Francis into an oratory, and in 1281 he embellished the exterior with a large arch. About the begining of the fourteenth century the Latin inscription was carved on the outside of the Gothic portal which reads: «This is the oratory at one time a stall for oxen and donkeys in which Francis, the mirror of the world was born». In the interior there are frescoes superimposed on each other dating from the end of the thirteenth and from the two succeeding centuries.

CHIESA NUOVA. Leaving the oratory and returning to Via Mazzini and proceeding in the direction of the Piazza del Comune, one can see on the left the Chiesa Nuova. «After the construction of the great churches of the thirteenth and fourteenth century, after the few chapels had been built in the fifteenth century, no other churches besides this one, the Chiesa Nuova, were erected. This church was built in 1615 on the site where according to tradition stood the house of Peter Bernardone» (E. Zocca).

S. Francesco Piccolino (St. Francis' birth-place)

CATHEDRAL OF SAN RUFINO. This edifice in Romanesque style is the work of Giovanni da Gubbio, begun in 1140. The façade is richly ornamented with symbolic sculptures, three portals, three rose windows variously decorated, and the bell tower. Beyond question this is one of the most noble façades of Romanesque style in Umbria. The interior, for structural reasons, was transformed according to the design of G. Alessi in the years 1571-1578.

Cathedral of San Rufino

In the side nave on the right is the Baptismal Font (originally in S. Maria Maggiore) where Francis and his first followers, St. Clare, Frederic of Svevia and St. Gabriel were baptized. The chapel of the Blessed Sacrament contains frescoes by Giorgetti, Carboni and Ciro Ferri. At the altar of Our Lady of Sorrows is an oil painting by dono Doni. There is a tryptich portraying various saints done by Niccolò Alunno in the fifteenth century which is found in the angle of the ceiling between the right nave and the central one. Above on the side altar to the right of the main altar is the Deposition from the Cross by Dono Doni in the sixteenth century. In the sacristy we find paintings of lesser value. In the apse the choir stalls are by Gian Giacomo da S. Severino (1450). At the end of the left nave the Chapel of the Madonna del Pianto, erected in 1894, and a Pieta carved out of wood, of German origin dating from the fifteenth century. In 1499 this image shed tears. Beneath the main altar is the tomb of San Rufino.
Near the exit near the base of the bell tower is a Roman cistern.
The Cathedral Museum contains illuminated choral books, one of which is perhaps the work of Oderisi da Gubbio, silverware of the twelfth to the fifteenth centuries among which the very beautiful tryptich taken away from San Rufinuccio done by Puccio Capanna, previously attributed to Stefano Fiorentino, the tryptich by Niccolo Alunno, and other paintings by Umbrian masters.
The crypt is interesting because it is all that remains of a Basilica which once stood here. One may see the traces of frescoes of the eleventh century, and a Roman sarcophagus in which rested the remains of S. Rufino.

ROCCA MAGGIORE OR THE FORTRESS. Upon leaving the piazza of San Rufino one may enter the street which forms an angle with the fountain, Via Porta Perlici in order to visit the Rocca Maggiore. History records this fortress in 1174. In 1198 it was destroyed by those in Assisi who rose in opposition to Corrado di Lutzen at the time that Frederick II of Svevia, was living there. After that time only temporary repairs were made up until the time the fortress was basically and completely restored by Albornoz (1363-1367). Additions to the structure were made from time to time until 1538.

Baptismal font

Chathedral of San Rufino: «*Pietà*» (German Art of the 15th cent.)

Hermitage « Le Carceri »

LE CARCERI. This hermitage, this sacred palace of retirement, was given by the Benedictines to St. Francis and his friars as a place of recollection and contemplation. The little convent and church adjacent to the original Cappella della Madonna (of the twelfth century) were erected by St. Bernardine of Siena. In the cloister is a well which according to tradition began to yield water at the prayer of St. Francis. One passes through the little chapel built by St. Bernardine, and then through the more rustic and devotional one of the Madonna, in order to descend to the grotto where St. Francis dwelt during his periods of retreat toward the end of his life. In the surrounding woods are other grottos used by the disciples of St. Francis.
Upon reentering the city one may go to the Piazza di S. Chiara to visit the Church of St. Clare.

BASILICA OF ST. CLARE. In general lines the structure imitates the upper church of the Basilica of St. Francis. Begun in 1257, four years after the death of St. Clare; the body of the Saint was buried here in 1260. The crypt in which rests the tomb of the Foundress of the Second Order of St. Francis, the Poor Clares, was constructed in 1850.
The rose window in the façade and the stained glass windows are modern imitations of classic works of art. The frescoes in the left wing of the transept depict scenes of the Old Testament and reveal the influence of Cimabue. The figures of saints in the four sections of the central vault above the main altar and the paintings of the New Testament, the Death of St. Clare in the right transept, are the work of an anonymous painter of the school of Giotto during the fourteenth century - called the Expressionistic Master of St. Clare.
Likewise in the right transept there is a Tavola depicting St. Clare and eight scenes from her life, a work done in 1283. It is the most ancient painting of the Saint made by an unknown Um-

Basilica of St. Clare

Basilica of St. Clare: Oil painting of St. Clare (1283)

brian artist who shows similarity to the Master di S. Francesco. Above the main altar is suspended a precious Crucifix, perhaps by the same artist to whom probably must be attributed the great Tavola (Maestà) in the left transept. Noteworthy is the fragmentary painting of the Nativity in this same transept by an anonymous Giottesco of the fourteenth century.

From the central nave one may enter the Chapel of the Crucifix where is exposed the precious Crucifix which spoke to St. Francis. In the rear of the chapel are various relics of St. Clare.

The adjoining Chapel of the Blessed Sacrament occupies the area of the ancient Church of St. George, in which Francis was instructed in the faith, and temporarily buried (1226-1230) and canonized (1228).

On the left wall a precious tryptich on wood, the Crucifixion and four saints by the same artist who painted the ceiling of St. Clare; a Polittico con Maestà and saints of Puccio Capanna (previously

lica of St. Clare: *Crucifix*
ch spoke to St. Francis (XIIth cent.)

Basilica of St. Clare: Crib: *Madonna with Child* - Detail (14th cent.)

Church of «S. Maria Maggiore» - Exterior

ascribed to Stefano Fiorentino); the Deposition from the Cross, Resurrection and Burial by an anonymous artist of the school of Giotto.
Descending along the Via S. Agnese some two hundred meters one comes upon the Oratory of St. Crispin, the seat of an ancient and important Confraternity (Arte dei Calzolai). The church, now turned into a garage, still has the trussed roof. The frescoes, done by a local collaborator of Giotto, are in the National Museum of Budapest; the more recent frescoes are in the Municipal Art Gallery.
In the beautiful Capitular Hall (today a storage place for the Ciammarughi house), there are still fragmentary decoration of Giottonean inspiration.
Over the portal is another fresco by a later painter of Giotto inspiration.
Farther along is the Piazza del Vescovado where St. Francis decisively renounced material possessions, giving up his inheritance rights, restoring to his father the very clothing he had on his back.

S. MARIA MAGGIORE. The plain rose window bears the date 1162 and the name Johannes, who ac-

cording to some critics is Giovanni da Gubbio who remodelled the façade of San Rufino.
The church was built on the ruins of a paleochristian temple, which in turn had been built on a preexisting pagan temple dedicate to Apollo. Recent excavations have brought to light fragments of Roman frescoes.
The interior has three naves. It was renovated in various stages, the most important seems to have been the work done in collaboration with St. Francis. On the walls are frescoes of the fourteenth and fifteenth centuries. In the crypt the columns bear Roman capitals which were perhaps taken from the ancient pagan temple, and a sarcophagus on which a cross is sculptured (ninth century).
Continuing along to the left on Via S. Apollinare which becomes Via Borgo S. Pietro one comes to the monastery of St. Joseph which is a combination of two manasteries: St. Apollinaris and St. Paul, each having its own chapel, which were originally separated by a lane.
In the interior of these churches transformed into halls (to see them, ring at the door of the Institute)

Church and Abbey of St. Peter (12th cent.)

there still remain fragments of precious frescoes by Puccio Capanna (previously ascribed to Stefano Fiorentino), among which is a Crucifixion and an Annunciation. The painting of the Stigmatization of St. Francis is the work of a helper of Puccio, and the picture of St. Apollinaris in throne is by an anonymous painter of the Giotto tradition.
Descending further along the way one comes to the Church of St. Peter, a Romanesque-Gothic structure built in 970, rebuilt in the thirteenth century. The rectangular façade with three entrances has three rose windows. The interior was restored in 1954. There are three naves in exposed stone with a raised sanctuary, a semicircular apse surmounted by a cupola. At the sides of the center entrance there are two tombs of the fourteenth century; there are four tombs dating from the fifteenth century at the sides of the sanctuary.
Here and there remain traces of frescoes of various epochs, fourteenth and fifteenth century. In the chapel of the left transept there is a precious tryptich on wood by Matteo da Gualdo.

S. DAMIANO. San Damiano is one of the places most sacred to the memory of the origins of Franciscanism. Here the Crucifix of which there is a copy above the altar spoke to St. Francis. Here Francis, after having enlarged the monastery, placed Sister Clare and the first Poor Clares in 1212.

Church of St. Damian

Choir of the Poor Clares

In front of the little church between the first arch and the portico is a painting of the Madonna with Child, and St. Francis, with the sponsor of the painting kneeling. It is a graceful fresco by an anonymous painter of the fourteenth century which is to be found also in the Chapel of St. George in St. Clare Church. Within the second arch St. Francis, St. Clare, St. Rocco and St. Sebastian painted by a less skilled artist of the fifteenth century.
At the side of the façade, by means of a window (Chapel of St. Jerome), one may observe a delicate fresco by Tiberio of Assisi (1517) done by order of Galeottus de Bistocchiis: in the center, the Virgin on throne with the Christchild; at the sides, St. Francis, St. Clare, St. Bernardine and St. Jerome. On the left wall: St. Rocco and St. Sebastian done by a pupil of Tiberio of Assisi in 1522.
In the interior of the church, immediately at the right, a fresco depicting two episodes in the life of St. Francis which happened at San Damiano: The father of St. Francis with a club in hand pursues him (the city of Assisi is seen in the background); St. Francis in prayer before the Crucifix. This fresco is to be ascribed to a local painter of the Giotto tradition of the fourteenth century, already a collaborator of the master who decorated the right transept of St. Clare Basilica.
In the adjacent chapel, a wooden Crucifix sculptured by Fra Innocenzo da Palermo (1637). In the calotte of

Refectory of the Poor Clares

the apse above the wooden choir of the fifteenth century, Madonna with Christ child between St. Damian and St. Rufino. Although very much retouched, this thirteenth century fresco is very gracious and shows evident signs of the Maestà del Cimabue in the lower Church of St. Francis.
From the little door at the left, passing through the cemetery of the Poor Clares one arrives at the little choir of St. Clare where are preserved the original stalls from the time of the Saint. On the right wall is the precious painting on wood of the Madonna with the Christ child and Friar Conradus done by a skilled painter of the Giotto tradition (perhaps Maestro del Farneto).
Ascending the narrow stairs from the burial place one passes the tiny garden of St. Clare and thence to the Oratory of the Saint where various relics are on display, among others a breviary written by Fra Leone and some frescoes of the second half of the fourteenth century, thence to the dormitory of the monastery of the Poor Clares.
Descending to the cloister where one may see two frescoes: The Annunciation and The Stigmatization (1507); they are the work of Eusebio da S. Giorgio. From the cloister one may enter the Refectory of the Poor Clares, most suggestive in its original condition. Frescoes by Dono Doni of the sixteenth century.

Cloister of St. Damian

Basilica of St. Mary of the Angels by Galcazzo Alessi 1596

S. MARIA DEGLI ANGELI. Erected in 1569, designed by Alessi. The neo-baroque façade by Bazzani was added some years ago. It houses the sacred little Chapel of the Porziuncola. This was the little church with the surrounding small piece (porziuncola) of land which the Benedictines of Monte Subasio gave in use to Francis and his friars, when they had been driven out of Rivotorto. The friars made the Porziuncola the place to which they returned after their apostolic voyages and missions. Of all the places where Francis stayed this is most closely connected with the memory of his apostolate and his holy life. Above the altar is the large polyptych by the priest Ilario da Viterbo (1393). Behind the little church of the Porziuncola, included today also in the Basilica, is the Cappella del Transito where St. Francis on the evening of Oct. 3, 1226 passed from this life to eternal life.

The Portiuncola: Exterior

In 1968 excavatIons had been made to the rear of the Porziuncola and a crypt was constructed to put in evidence the foundations of the ancient friary or the original Basilica, which had been removed to make room for the actual grandiose structure.
With the exception of the Crypt which contains terracotta panels of excellent artistic value done by Andrea della Robbia, the other chapels of the Basilica

Inside view of the Portiuncola

are ornamented with frescoes and oil paintings mostly by artists of the seventeenth century such as: Brozzini (Chapel of St. Anthony), Moretti (Chapel of St. Rufino), Ciburi, (Chapel of the Crowning of the Blessed Virgin), Sermei and Giorgetti (Chapel of the Stigmatization and Chapel of St. John the Baptist), Cavallucci and Garbi (Chapel of S. Diego), Pomarancio (Chapel of St. Ann), Zuccari and Baroccio (Chapel of the Nativity), Guerrini (Chapel of St. Peter of Alcantara).

From the church one may go visit the Roseto of St. Francis where according to tradition the Saint cast himself among the thorns to conquer severe temptations. Nearby is the Chapel of the Roses with frescoes by Tiberio of Assisi (1506-1516) containing the story of the Porziuncola Indulgence, inspired by the polyptych of Ilario, and Holy Men and Women of the Franciscan Order and St. Francis among his twelve first companions.
But the most important works of art are those kept in the Museum: A crucifix by Giunta Pisano; a painting on wood of St. Francis by the Maestro di S. Francesco; a second painting on wood of St. Francis by Cimabue; a Madonna with Child by the Sienese painter Sano di Pietro (fourteenth century); and a removed fresco of Madonna with Child and Angels, the work of Mezzastris (fifteenth century).
Worth visiting if possible is the large cloister containing the frescoes by Francesco Providoni (seventeenth century), and the two Refectories with the works of Dono Doni (sixteenth century) and of Providoni and Pomarancio.

Crypt of the Church: Polyptic in Terracotta by Andrea della Robbia

This sanctuary became renowned the world over because of the famous Indulgence called the Perdono di Assisi. In 1216 the Blessed Virgin Mary surrounded by a choir of angels (the sanctuary is dedicated to St. Mary of the Angels) appeared to St. Francis, and having heard his petitions, obtained from God the plenary indulgence for all those who would visit the Porziuncola; Pope Honorius III, recently elected, and the residing in nearby Perugia, gave his approval for this indulgence, which in those day could be gained only by the Crusaders who went to the Holy Land, and by the pious pilgrims who visited the tombs of the Apostles in Rome. For seven centuries milions and millions of pilgrims were able, thanks to St. Francis, to obtain this pardon of the punishments due to their sins.
In 1909 St. Pius X proclaimed this Franciscan sanctuary also «Caput et Mater» of the Minorite Order and elevated it to the dignity of Patriarchal Basilica and Cappella Papale, similar to the Basilica of St. Francis in Assisi which had altready for two centuries enjoyed these privileges ensuing from these titles.

Church of Rivotorto

THE TUGURIO OF RIVOTORTO. Along the main road to Rome, two kilometers distant from Santa Maria degli Angeli, is the stall of Rivotorto. It is the Cradle of the Franciscan Order. In the interior of the church, entirely reconstructed in neo-gothic style after the earthquake of 1894, 1,80 below the street level is the humble tugurio where Francis and his friars dwelt from 1209 to 1211. Like San Damiano and the Carceri, Rivotorto retains something of that aura of the early Franciscan origins. An inscription posted on the façade of the church says: «Here began the Order of the Friars Minor». Francis came here in 1209 with his first disciples, Bernard of Quintavalle and Pietro di Cattano, to whom quite soon others associated themselves. They remained here about two years, obtaining their food as the Poverello records in his spiritual Testament by the work of their hands, or not being able to do so, by recourse to the table of the Lord: alms. Here evolved the proposal to obtain juridical status for their group.
Thus in 1209 was formulated the first Rule and approved orally by Innocent III.
A trip to Assisi would not be complete perhaps, without a visit to ROCCA S. ANGELO (Rocchicciola) only 11 kilometers away. To get there one should take the road to Petrignano.

The interior of the little church of S. Maria in Arce (today juridically dependent upon the Basilica of St. Francis in Assisi) contains many works of art from which this small rural town derives its importance. It was also the reason for the constant preoccupation and past visits of the Danish writer and poet Johannes Joergensen.

The Tugurio of Rivotorto «the first home of the Franciscans» (1209-1211)

In the church are found devotional frescoes by Spagna, Bart. Caporali, Matteo da Gualdo, Dono Doni and many other minor painters of the fifteenth and sixteenth centuries.
The most important and pleasant surprise of all are the giottesque frescoes of the first decades of the fourteenth century: The Stigmata (fragment) by Maestro di Figline (Giovanni di Bonino?); The Presentation at the Temple, Flight into Egypt, Disputation among the Doctors (apse), and the Maestà with Saints by Maestro Espressionista di S. Chiara.

Church of Rocca S. Angelo - Interior

2 - Town Hall Square - Church of St. Mary above Minerva
3 - St. Francis' birth place
4 - The Basilica of St. Clare
5 - The Cathedral of St. Rufino
6 - Rocca Maggiore
7 - The Hermitage of the Carceri
8 - St. Mary Major and the Bishop's Residence
9 - Pro Civitate Christiana
10 - The Abbey Church of St. Peter
11 - San Damiano
12 - Rivotorto
13 - Basilica of St. Mary of the Angels
O
E
S
PORTA S. GIACOMO
PIAZZA SUPERIORE S. FRANCESCO
PORTA S. FRANCESCO
PORTA S. PIETRO
PIAZZA S. PIETRO
VIA SAN FRANCESCO
VIA DEL FOSSO CUPO
VIA BORGO S. PIETRO
VIA DEL SEMENTONE
VIA S. APOLLINARE
PORTA DEL SEMENTONE
VIALE VITTORIO EMANUELE II
GUGLIELMO MARCONI
PIAZZA DEL COMUNE
PIAZZA S. RUFINO
PIAZZA MATTEOTTI
VIA GALEAZZO ALESSI
PORTA PERLICI
PORTA CAPPUCCINI
km. 5
PORTA MOIANO
BASILICA DI S. CHIARA
BORGO ARETINO
VIALE UMBERTO I
PORTA NUOVA
S. DAMIANO
RIVOTORTO
BASILICA DI S. MARIA DEGLI ANGELI
PERUGIA - FIRENZE
FOLIGNO - ROMA